AF601287

NORSE MYTHOLOGY

VALKYRIES

BY HEATHER C. HUDAK

Kids Core

An Imprint of Abdo Publishing
abdobooks.com

abdobooks.com

Published by Abdo Publishing, a division of ABDO, PO Box 398166, Minneapolis, Minnesota 55439.

Printed in the United States of America, North Mankato, Minnesota.
052023
092023

Cover Photos: Shutterstock Images (Valkyrie, horse, background)
Interior Photos: Historica Graphica Collection/Heritage Images/Hulton Archive/Getty Images, 4–5; Fine Art Images/Heritage Images/Hulton Fine Art Collection/Getty Images, 7, 12, 14–15, 28 (top), 29 (bottom); Lieberenz/ullstein bild/Getty Images, 8; Fine Art Images/Heritage Image Partnership Ltd/Alamy, 11; Arthur Rackham/The Rhinegold & the Valkyrie/Wikimedia Commons, 16, 29 (top); Morten Andreassen/Shutterstock Images, 19 (building); Pierre Chaton, 19 (hall); Shutterstock Images, 19 (spears), 19 (cook), 19 (goat), 20; Eric Isselee/Shutterstock Images, 19 (deer); Olga Ozik/Shutterstock Images, 19 (chain mail, rightmost); Brandon Bourdages/Shutterstock Images, 19 (chain mail); IG Digital Arts/Shutterstock Images, 19 (boar); Ivy Close Images/Alamy, 21, 28 (bottom); Photo12/Jasin Boland/Walt Disney Pictures/Marvel Studios/Alamy, 22–23; SHM Employee/Swedish History Museum, https://mis.historiska.se/mis/sok/bild.asp?uid=22806, 25; Kiselev Andrey Valerevich/Shutterstock Images, 26

Editor: Katharine Hale
Series Designer: Katharine Hale

Library of Congress Control Number: 2022949121

Publisher's Cataloging-in-Publication Data

Names: Hudak, Heather C., author.
Title: Valkyries / by Heather C. Hudak
Description: Minneapolis, Minnesota: Abdo Publishing Company, 2024 | Series: Norse mythology | Includes online resources and index.
Identifiers: ISBN 9781098291235 (lib. bdg.) | ISBN 9781098277413 (ebook)
Subjects: LCSH: Mythology, Norse--Juvenile literature. | Valkyries (Norse mythology)--Juvenile literature. | Divinities--Juvenile literature.
Classification: DDC 293.13--dc23

CONTENTS

In some stories, Brunhild is Odin's daughter.

CHAPTER 1

BRUNHILD AND SIGURD

Valkyries were mighty warrior women. They served Odin, the leader of the Norse gods. He would send the Valkyries into battles. They decided who lived and died while fighting.

Brunhild was a Valkyrie. She was known for her beauty.

One day, she killed a king during a battle. Odin had promised victory to that king. Odin was angry with Brunhild. He said she could no longer fight. She had to get married. But Brunhild had sworn to marry only a fearless man.

Odin cursed Brunhild to sleep. He sent her to a faraway castle surrounded by shields. A brave hero named Sigurd found her there.

Valkyries and Swans

Some stories associate Valkyries with swans. Valkyries wear swan skins or clothes made of feathers. A person can control a Valkyrie by stealing her feathers. In one poem, Brunhild says a king controlled her by stealing her cloak. He made Brunhild kill the king Odin favored in battle, which caused her punishment.

Sigurd is called Siegfried in Germanic mythology.

He cut through the **chain mail** she wore, and she woke up. Brunhild told Sigurd her story. She taught him the power of **runes**. For example, carving victory runes on his sword would bring him victory. Sigurd was impressed with Brunhild's wisdom. The two promised to get married.

A set of four operas called *The Ring of the Nibelung* tells the story of Sigurd and Brunhild.

Sigurd traveled to another kingdom. The queen had a daughter, Gudrun. The queen thought Sigurd would be a good husband for Gudrun. She gave Sigurd a magic drink. It made him forget about Brunhild. Sigurd married Gudrun. He swore an **oath** of brotherhood with her brothers, Gunnar and Hogni. The queen told Gunnar he should marry Brunhild.

Brunhild had surrounded her home with a ring of fire. She said she would marry only a man brave enough to cross the flames. Sigurd and Gunnar rode there together. Gunnar tried to cross the flames. But his horse would not move. Sigurd's horse would not let Gunnar ride him. So, Sigurd made himself look like Gunnar with magic. Then he broke through the fire. Brunhild was disappointed. She had thought only Sigurd would be able to break the ring of fire. But she agreed to marry Gunnar.

Later, Brunhild learned the truth. She was heartbroken. She was also angry. She told Gunnar to kill Sigurd. She told him he would lose everything, including her, if he did not. Gunnar had sworn an oath of brotherhood with Sigurd. But his youngest brother had not. Gunnar convinced his brother to kill Sigurd. When Brunhild heard the news, she stabbed herself with a sword. She asked to be placed on the same funeral **pyre** as Sigurd. That way, they could be together forever in the afterlife.

Norse Mythology

Valkyries were part of epic stories known today as Norse mythology. These stories came from the religious beliefs of early northern

Valkyries are warriors from Norse mythology.

Germanic peoples. Norse mythology dates back to the 600s CE or even earlier. The stories were passed down through the generations. They were told out loud. As a result, they changed over time. They were not written down until hundreds of years later. This means the surviving myths might not match what the Norse people believed. Most surviving Norse myths come from **Scandinavia**.

Valkyries played an important role in battle.

Myths were used to explain events, such as bad weather or a good harvest. Norse mythology tells of gods and goddesses, dragons, dwarfs, giants, and people. Brunhild is one of many Valkyries in Norse mythology.

Gripisspa is an Old Norse poem. In this poem, Sigurd's uncle **foretells** what will happen between Sigurd and Brunhild. Sigurd replies:

> This is the worst,
> that I must court
> the famous woman
> I love most of all
> to be the fair bride
> of another man.

Source: Jackson Crawford, translator. *The Poetic Edda: Stories of the Norse Gods and Heroes*. Hackett, 2015, p. 229.

What's the Big Idea?

What is this quote's main idea? Explain how the main idea is supported by details.

Valkyries took fallen warriors to Valhalla. This place is described as a warrior's paradise.

CHAPTER 2

LOYAL CAREGIVERS

In early Norse myths, Valkyries were demons. They fed on dead soldiers. Later, their image changed. They became caregivers and warriors. Valkyries were beautiful women. Some were mythical beings. Others were human.

Valkyries wore armor and carried spears.

They were the daughters of kings and heroes and were given special powers.

Valkyries served Odin. He gave them shining armor. It made the Valkyries look like beams of light so humans couldn't see them. Valkyries wore helmets and chain mail. They carried spears and shields. They rode on flying horses. Valkyries went with soldiers into battle and watched over them. Sometimes, Valkyries even fought in battles.

Guides to the Afterlife

The word *Valkyrie* means "chooser of the **slain**." Valkyries were given this name because they decided the fate of soldiers in battle. Valkyries were known for guiding the souls of fallen soldiers to the afterlife. But they did not take all of the soldiers. Freya was a powerful goddess. She chose half of the soldiers. They came to Freya's hall called Sessrumnir. Valkyries brought the other fallen heroes to a place called Valhalla.

Valhalla was a huge hall where the soldiers lived. Odin made sure the soldiers were happy.

He made sure they wanted for nothing. Odin needed the soldiers to help him at Ragnarok. *Ragnarok* was the term the Norse people used to describe the end of the world. The soldiers practiced fighting during the day. At night, they feasted with Odin. They ate **boar** and had an endless supply of drinks.

Norse Afterlife

There are some clues in surviving myths to help explain what Norse people believed about the afterlife. Warriors could be chosen for Valhalla or Sessrumnir. Most other people went to Hel. This place was foggy and dark, but the dead were treated well. Aegir is a giant or god who represents the sea. Ran is his wife. Some stories say people who die at sea end up in her land.

Valhalla
A Warrior's Paradise
Gold shields on the roof
Magical goat Heithrun
Provides endless drinks from her udder
Deer Eikthyrnir
Antlers drip water that creates a spring from which all rivers flow
Spears for rafters
540 doors
Hundreds of warriors can march through each
Andhrimnir
Cook of the gods who prepares meals
Great boar Saehrimnir
After being eaten, it returns to its full size
Benches covered in chain mail

Odin's warriors will fight at Ragnarok.

Odin's warriors spent their days fighting and their nights feasting.

In their free time, Valkyries were hostesses in Valhalla. They served the soldiers. They made sure the soldiers' souls were taken care of in the afterlife.

Further Evidence

Visit the website below. Does it give any new information about Norse afterlife beliefs that wasn't in Chapter Two?

Viking Burial

abdocorelibrary.com/valkyries

Tessa Thompson plays the character Valkyrie in the Marvel Cinematic Universe.

WARRIOR WOMEN

Valkyries were both worshipped and feared, especially by soldiers. If Odin wanted someone to win a battle, Valkyries could make it happen. The Valkyries carried out Odin's wishes. They could also protect soldiers.

They sometimes shielded soldiers in battle. They could also come to soldiers in dreams to bring them warnings. Soldiers prayed they would be taken to Valhalla if they died.

Supporting Role

Valkyries were not often the main characters in Norse myths. They played a supporting role.

Superhero Valkyrie

Marvel Comics introduced a superhero named Valkyrie in 1970. She is also known as Brunnhilde. She leads a group of warrior women called the Valkyrior. A version of this character also appears in the Marvel Cinematic Universe. Tessa Thompson plays Valkyrie in *Thor: Ragnarok*, *Avengers: Endgame*, and *Thor: Love and Thunder*.

Historians have found Valkyrie pendants in Scandinavia, including these four from Sweden.

But they were still an important part of Norse mythology. Valkyries were portrayed in pendants, carvings, drawings, poems, and songs.

Myths about Valkyries might be based on real-life shield-maidens. These women fought alongside men in battles.

In 2012, a small figurine of a woman was found in Harby, Denmark. It was made of silver and dated back to about 800 CE. The woman carried a sword and shield. She had a ponytail and a beautiful outfit. Historians think the figure might represent a Valkyrie.

Tales of Valkyries' beauty and bravery have been passed down for hundreds of years. People still tell stories about them today. They live on in operas, comics, movies, and more.

Helgakvitha Hundingsbana I is an Old Norse poem. It tells the story of Helgi, who wins a Valkyrie's hand in marriage. The poem says:

He saw Valkyries
wearing helmets
in the high heavens;
their armor was bloody
and banners waved
from their spears.

Source: Jackson Crawford, translator. *The Poetic Edda: Stories of the Norse Gods and Heroes.* Hackett, 2015, pp. 192–193.

Comparing Texts

Does this quote support the information in this chapter? Or does it give a different perspective?

LEGENDARY FACTS

The word *Valkyrie* means "chooser of the slain."

Freya chose half of all fallen soldiers for Sessrumnir. Valkyries guided the rest to Valhalla.

Valkyries wore armor and carried spears and shields.

Brunhild was the most beautiful and famous of the Valkyries.

Glossary

boar
a wild pig

chain mail
protective mesh made from small circles of metal

foretells
predicts ahead of time what will happen in the future

oath
a serious promise

pyre
a pile of wood used to build a fire

runes
alphabetic symbols used by the Norse people and believed to have special powers

Scandinavia
the countries of Norway, Sweden, and Denmark, and sometimes Iceland and Finland

slain
killed in a violent way

Online Resources

To learn more about Valkyries, visit our free resource websites below.

Visit **abdocorelibrary.com** or scan this QR code for free Common Core resources for teachers and students, including vetted activities, multimedia, and booklinks, for deeper subject comprehension.

Visit **abdobooklinks.com** or scan this QR code for free additional online weblinks for further learning. These links are routinely monitored and updated to provide the most current information available.

Learn More

Alexander, Heather. *A Child's Introduction to Norse Mythology*. Black Dog & Leventhal, 2018.

Conley, Kate. *Odin*. Abdo, 2024.

Rea, Amy C. *Dragons of Norse Mythology*. Abdo, 2024.

Index

About the Author

Heather C. Hudak has written hundreds of kids' books on all kinds of topics. She loves to travel when she's not writing. Hudak has traveled all over the world, including Germany and Scandinavia. She also enjoys camping with her husband and many pets.